Kale Cookbook

Easy, Healthy and Delicious Kale Recipes to

Live Longer and Feel Younger

DINGO
BOOK CLUB

"Great Books Change Life"

Table of Contents

Introduction

Consuming the right combination of vegetables, fruits, cereals, and spices on a regular basis would reduce the risk of these common disorders. In our busy lifestyle where we don't have time to follow traditional cooking methods or recipes, we don't usually pay attention to what our body wants and end up eating a lot of processed food and junk items. Though we try to keep ourselves healthy by planning to follow a rigid exercise routine and strict diet, we never usually implement them due to our strenuous lifestyle. One of the easiest and simplest ways to be healthy is by adding Kale to your diet. They are simple, healthy and delicious with rich nutrition benefits.

Kale is one of the most nutrient dense commonly available foods anywhere on Earth. It is very low in calories and contains very little fat. Belonging to the cabbage family (Bassic oleracea), kale comes in many different types with leaves that can be purple or green with either a curly or smooth shape. It is related to broccoli, cauliflower, Brussels sprouts and collard greens.

In one serving of raw kale (1 cup) about 2.4 oz. or 67 grams, there are 33 calories, 6 grams of carbohydrates and 3 grams of protein. It also contains 684% of the recommended daily amount of Vitamin K1, 206% of Vitamin A, 134%of Vitamin C, 9% of Vitamin B6 and at least 3% of Thiamin (V B1), Riboflavin (V B2), and Niacin (V B3) as well as Iron and Phosphorus. Plus, 26% of the recommended amount of Manganese 10% of Copper, 9 % of Calcium and Potassium, plus 6% of Magnesium.

Kale is full of compounds that are known to have protective effects against many of today's chronic diseases such as cancer, heart disease, high blood, diabetes and respiratory conditions.

To make your life simpler, we have also compiled a wide array of recipes that use Kales so you can adapt these power bombs in your daily diet.

I hope this book serves as an informative and interesting read to you!

Happy Reading!

Chapter 1:

Smoothie's and Juices

Kale, Banana, Pineapple & Almond Milk Smoothie

Makes 2 servings

Raw Kale with its slightly bitter, tangy taste is matched perfectly in this smoothie where the flavors work together to complement each other. Bananas can be peeled and sliced then frozen before adding, to make a super cool smoothie.

Ingredients

- 1 cup of chopped and well packed down Kale Leaves
- 1 cup of unsweetened Almond Milk
- ½ a cup of fresh Pineapple Juice
- ½ cup fresh diced Pineapple
- 1 medium ripe Banana

Directions

Place all of the ingredients in your blender or food processor and blend them on high until smooth.

Kale, Blackberry and Chocolate Smoothie

Makes 4 servings

This mouth-watering smoothie combines kale and the high protein of chocolate whey powder with the richness of almond butter and the goodness of blackberries, coconut and bananas.

Ingredients

- 6 to 7 large Kale Leaves, with their hard stork removed then sliced to fit your blender
- 2 medium peeled and sliced frozen Bananas
- 3 tbsp of Chocolate Protein Powder
- 2 cups of Coconut Milk
- ½ a cup of unsweetened shredded Coconut
- 1 tbsp of Almond Butter
- ½ a cup of frozen Blackberries (or berries of your choice)
- ½ a cup of fresh water to use as needed

Directions

Place all of the ingredients in your blender or food processor and blend them on high until smooth.

Kale, High Calcium Smoothie

Makes 2 servings

This is super high calcium and antioxidant smoothie is great for everyone to round off the diet and detox.

Ingredients

- 1 cup of packed Baby Kale
- 1/3 of a cup of Parsley

- 6 medium Carrots
- 4 stalks of Celery with leaves
- 1 whole Cucumber
- 1 whole Green Apple Seeds and skin included
- ½ inch piece of Green Ginger

Directions

Place all of the ingredients in your blender or food processor and blend them on high until smooth.

Tips on using Kale in smoothies

Kale is easy to freeze to maintain in optimum condition for using in your smoothies at any time. Cut away the hard rib from the leaves and give it a good rinse. Then freeze it. This helps to make it taste less bitter and also cool down your smoothie.

Or if preferred it can be blanched until soft before freezing. This will help to break down its cellular structure, increasing its digestibility and helping you to easily absorb its many nutrients.

Chapter 2: Snacks

Kale can be used in many ways to make super healthy snacks; the following recipes are easy, quick and satisfying.

Savory Kale Chips

Makes a snack for 3 to 4 people

Kale chips are a very popular snack which can make a healthy alternative to conventional processed potato chips.

Ingredients

- A good sized bunch of Fresh Kale Leaves
- 1 tbsp of Coconut or good quality Olive Oil

For the spice

- 1.5 tbsp of Nutritional Yeast
- 1 tsp of Garlic Powder
- ¾ of a tsp of Red Chili Powder
- ½ a tsp of Onion Powder
- ½ a tsp of Smoked Paprika
- ¼ of a tsp of Black Cumin Powder
- ¼ of a tsp of Ground Celery Seeds
- ¼ of a tsp of fine Sea Salt
- 1/8 of a tsp of Cayenne Pepper

Directions

1. Preheat your oven to 300F
2. Line a large baking tray or 2 with parchment paper
3. Take the hard stem from the kale leaves and tear the leaves into bite sized pieces

4. Thoroughly wash the leaves and then dry them completely. This can be done with paper towels or a lettuce spinner, but the leaves must be dry - otherwise they will steam and become soggy

5. Place the dried leaves in a large bowl and add the oil, massaging into into all parts of the leaves

6. Mix all the spice ingredients together and sprinkle over the leaves then toss to combine and cover the leaves

7. Spread the leaves out in one layer on the parchment paper. Ensure the leaves are not overcrowded, so they will bake rather than steam

8. Bake the kale for about 10 minutes, then turn the leaves and bake for about another 10 to 15 minutes or until they become firm. Note they will have shrunk and when removed from the oven will continue to firm up on the trays if left for about 3 minutes.

9. Cook them as required as they need to be consumed straight away rather than stored, because they will lose their crispness quickly.

10. Do not add any liquids before cooking as this will cause them to steam rather than bake and result in soggy limp leaves. If you wish to add a liquid seasoning, do so after they are cooked or use as a dipping sauce.

Kale and Toasted Walnut Pesto

Makes about 4 servings

This tasty pesto can be used as a dip, a spread or added to your favorite pasta to make wholesome meal.

Ingredients

- 2 cups of fresh packed Kale with the stems removed
- 1 cup of fresh Basil Leaves
- ½ a cup of freshly shaved or grated Parmesan Cheese
- 1/3 of a cup of freshly toasted Walnuts
- 4 to 6 cloves of fresh chopped Garlic
- ¼ of a cup of Extra Virgin Olive Oil
- 1 tsp of fine Sea Salt

Directions

1. Place the kale leaves, basil and salt in your blender or food processor and pulse until they are finely shredded.
2. With the motor running on medium, slowly pour the olive oil until combined
3. Scrape the sides of the processor and add the garlic and walnuts and pulse again until combined.
4. If you are using straight away add the Parmesan now or wait until just before using for the best results

Crisp Kale Bars

Makes 10 medium sized bars

These crispy kale bars are great for school snacks or for snacks when in the great outdoors.

Ingredients

- A large bunch of fresh Kale
- 1 tbsp of Coconut Oil
- 1 cup of Quick Cooking Oats
- 1/3 of a cup of Sunflower or Pumpkin Seeds
- 2 tbsp of Sunflower Seeds
- 1 cup puffed Whole Grain Cereal such as Quinoa or Rice
- 1/3 of a cup of dried Berries such as Cherries, Cranberries etc.
- 1/3 of a cup of Almond or Cashew Butter
- ¼ of a cup of Natural Organic Cane Sugar
- ¼ of a cup of Raw Honey, Maple Syrup of Molasses
- ¼ of a tsp of fine Sea Salt
- ¼ of a tsp of Vanilla or Almond Extract

Direction

1. Preheat your oven to 300F
2. Line an 8 inch square pan with parchment paper and lightly brush it with coconut oil to stop the kale sticking

3. Prepare the kale by removing the hard stems and then washing it well in water.

4. Completely dry the kale with paper towels or in a lettuce spinner

5. Then place them in a bowl with the oil and massage the oil over all parts of the leaves to coat

6. Bake the kale for about 15 minutes or until the leaves have shrunk and become firm. Do not allow them to become brown. Once cooked, remove on the parchment and cool

7. Bake the oats and seeds in the oven until they are fragrant and golden

8. Transfer the oats and seeds to a mixing bowl and combine with the berries and cereal

9. Crumble the cooled kale leaves into the mixture and stir to combine

10. Place the nut butter, sugar, honey and salt in a heavy bottomed saucepan and heat them on a low to medium heat until the sugar is dissolved and the mixture is smooth. Then remove it from the heat and stir in the extract

11. While still hot, pour the nut butter and sugar mixture over the oats and stir to combine, then pour the whole mixture into your prepared dish as in instruction 1

12. Oil a sheet of plastic film and place in on top of the mixture in your pan and use this to spread and compress the mixture evenly

13. When the mixture is flat and even place it in the refrigerator to cool and set for several hours

14. Remove the mixture from the pan using the parchment paper and cut it on a cutting board into 10 even sized bars. Then wrap them individually in plastic before storing in your refrigerator for up to a week or 3 months in the freezer

Kale and Chocolate Cookies

Makes about a dozen cookies the recipe can be doubled

Kale and chocolate are a great combination, rounded out with a touch of vanilla in this wheat free gluten free recipe.

Ingredients

- 1 cup of Oat Flour
- 1 cup of packed raw Kale with the stems removed
- 1/3 of a cup of Chocolate Chips
- ½ a cup of Raw Sugar
- 2 tbsp of Whole Milk or Nut Milk
- 2 tbsp of Coconut Oil or Ghee
- ¼ of a tsp of pure Vanilla Extract
- ½ a tsp of Baking Soda
- ¼ of a tsp of fine Sea Salt

Directions

1. Place all the dry ingredients except for the kale in a bowl and mix to aerate and combine
2. Wash and rinse the kale, then slice it very finely or process in your food processor
3. Place the wet ingredients with the kale in a separate bowl and stir to combine then fold the wet ingredients into the dry mixture.
4. Mix it until you have a nice dough consistency

5. Preheat your oven to 350F and oil a baking tray.
6. Roll the dough into about a dozen equal sized balls and place them on the baking tray
7. Bake for about 11 minutes, then allow to cool before eating

Chapter 3: Salads

Salads are without a doubt one of the tastiest and simplest ways to provide your family with the majority of nutrients they require. Using the superfood kale in your salads brings them to a new level. Salads with kale benefit by being made several hours before serving so the dressing can bring out the flavors and soften the kale.

Greek Kale and Avocado Salad

Makes 8 servings

This hearty and colorful salad is an ideal addition to compliment any dish or even a complete meal on its own, especially if you add some cooked chicken or seafood.

Ingredients

- 4 cups of fresh Kale leaves with their stems removed then torn into bite sized pieces
- 1 large Avocado, peeled, stoned and sliced
- 1 medium Cucumber, diced
- 1 cup of ripe Cherry Tomatoes, sliced in half
- 1 medium Red Pepper, deseeded and sliced thinly
- 1 medium Green Pepper, deseeded and sliced thinly
- 1 medium Red Onion, Sliced thinly
- 1 cup of Artichoke Hearts, halved
- ¼ of a cup of Green Olives
- ¼ of a cup of Black Olives
- ½ a cup of Fresh chopped Basil or 2 tsp of dried
- ½ a cup of fresh Feta Cheese, diced or crumbled

The Dressing

1. ¼ of a cup of Olive Oil or 50/50 Olive and Avocado Oils
2. The juice of one Lemon or lemon and Lime

3. 1 of a tsp of Dried Oregano

4. ½ of a tsp of Dried Basil

5. ¼ of a tsp of Dried Thyme

6. ½ of a tsp of Garlic Powder

7. ¼ of a tsp of Freshly Cracked Black Pepper

8. ¼ of a tsp of Sea Salt

Directions

Place all the dressing ingredients in a bowl and whisk them together and allow them to infuse while making the salad

Combine all the salad ingredients in a large bowl and toss them with the dressing

Kale and Garlic Sauerkraut

Makes about 4 to 6 servings

Sauerkrauts are very low calorie foods and this version is packed full of anti-inflammatory compounds as well as probiotics and dietary fiber.

Ingredients

- 1 small whole Cabbage, finely shredded
- 2 or 3 whole outer Cabbage Leaves
- 6 cups of finely sliced Kale
- 6 cloves of Garlic, crushed
- ½ a bunch of chopped Green Spring Onions
- ½ a grated carrot
- ½ a tsp of finely diced Red Chili (optional)

Directions

1. Place all the ingredients, apart from the 2 or 3 extra cabbage leaves, in a heavy bowl and pound them with a wooden hammer or kraut pounder until the release their juices and soften. (about 5 to 6 minutes)
2. Place all the vegetables and their juices in a large jar. It is important that there are no air gaps so press them in firmly. If you need more juice to cover either juice some extra cabbage or add a little salted water

3. Fill the jar to about 1 inch below the top and use the extra cabbage leaves to cover the top of the vegetables. Ensure there is no air trapped under the leaves and that juice is covering the top

4. Place the lid on tightly to keep unwanted visitors out and set the jar in a spot where it will not be disturbed and out of direct sunlight.

5. The kraut will take from 5 to 10 days to ferment depending on the temperature in your house. Each day you need to loosen the top to vent any gasses.

6. When the initial ferment is finished, you can eat it or allow it to keep fermenting. Place it in the fridge where it will keep for up to 12 months.

Kale, Apple, Almond and Cheddar Salad with Fresh Parsley

Makes a salad for 2 people

A quick and refreshing, tasty salad that's perfect for a slimming lunch

Ingredients

- 4 cups of Curly Kale, finely sliced
- 2 tbsp of coarsely chopped roasted Nuts of your choice
- 1 whole Green Apple, diced
- 1.5 ounces of Extra Tasty Cheddar, cut into ¼ inch cubes
- 1 tbsp of Fresh Lemon Juice
- 1 tbsp of Fresh Lime Juice
- 1 clove of minced Garlic
- 2 tbsp of freshly shaved Parmesan Cheese
- 5 tbsp of Extra Virgin Olive Oil
- 3 tbsp of fresh, finely chopped Parsley
- Sea Salt and freshly cracked Black Pepper to taste

Directions

1. Combine together the kale, apple, almonds and cheddar in a large serving bowl
2. Whisk the lemon, lime, olive oil, garlic and salt together and toss it into the salad turning to evenly coat everything.
3. Sprinkle the parmesan and parsley over the top and serve

Chapter 4:

Kale Breakfasts Ideas

Kale is an ingredient not normally associated with breakfasts, but it is actually a very versatile vegetable and can be incorporated into many dishes.

Kale and Mozzarella Scrambled Eggs

Makes 2 servings

You can substitute any type of cheese for the mozzarella if you prefer and, if inclined, you can select any herb combination that suits your taste.

Ingredients

- 1 cup of finely sliced Kale with the stems removed
- 4 large fresh Eggs, lightly beaten
- ½ cup of Mozzarella Cheese or your own choice
- ¼ cup of finely diced Onion
- ½ tsp of Italian Seasoning
- A medium pinch of Red Chili Powder
- 1 tsp of Coconut Oil or Ghee
- Sea Salt and freshly cracked Black Pepper

Directions

1. Sautee the onion in a heavy bottomed pan on a high heat with the oil and chili powder
2. Add the kale to the pan and continue sautéing until it's wilted
3. Turn the heat to medium low and add the beaten eggs. Stirring until they start to set, then stir in the cheese. Stir until all is well combined and season with salt and pepper, then serve.

Kale and Sweet Potato Fritters

Makes 18 to 20 mini patties or serving for 4 people

With a crispy exterior and soft, creamy interior, these tasty little fritters are full of vitamins and flavor, a breakfast treat with a spicy dip and your style of eggs, making a filling breakfast

Ingredients

- 2 cups of finely sliced Kale with stalks removed
- 3 cups of pureed, steamed, Sweet Potato
- 2 cups of cooked Quinoa
- 2 fresh Eggs
- 3 tbsp of Cornstarch
- ½ a cup of Bread Crumbs or Ground Oats
- 1 tsp of grated Ginger
- ¼ of a tsp of Smoked Paprika, ground
- 1 tsp of freshly cracked Black Pepper
- 1 tsp Of Sea Salt
- ¼ of a cup of Coconut Oil or Ghee

For the Dipping Sauce

- ¼ of a cup of Yogurt
- 1 tsp of freshly grated Ginger
- 2 tbsp of Chili Sauce
- Sea Salt and Cracked Black Pepper to taste

Directions

1. Place all the ingredients in a mixing bowl and combine well, then allow them to sit for 10 minutes

2. Heat a medium sized, heavy bottomed, fry pan on a medium heat with the coconut oil

3. Using a tablespoon, scoop up the mixture from the bowl and place it into the hot oil cooking about 5 to 6 at a time. Slightly flatten each fritter and cook them for 3 to 4 minutes each side or until they are golden brown.

4. They can be served hot, warm or at room temperature

Kale and Tofu Basket

Makes 2 servings

This nutritious mixture of vegetables gives you a high powered protein and vitamin breakfast to last the whole morning so you don't feel the need to snack until lunch time.

Ingredients

- 6 to 8 large Kale leaves with the hard ribs removed and torn into bite sized pieces
- 12 ounces of extra firm Tofu, (marinated or plain), cut into ¾ inch cubes
- ½ a cup of Pickled Cabbage or Sauerkraut
- 2 tbsp of Nutritional Yeast
- 1 to 2 tbsp of Coconut Oil
- Some coarse Sea Salt

Optional toppings

- Sun-dried Tomatoes, Mushrooms, Aubergines, Mushrooms or Fruit of your choice
- Radishes thinly sliced
- Kale Pesto
- Nut Crème or Butter
- A poached Organic Egg
- Sliced Avocado
- Tomato, Chili, or Salsa

Directions

1. Place a little coconut oil in a large, heavy bottomed pan and heat it to a medium temperature
2. Sprinkle the tofu with the coarse salt and sauté it in the hot oil until golden brown, about 7 minutes, keep stirring and brown on all sides
3. Once browned, sprinkle the yeast over the tofu and stir it so it is evenly coated
4. Then lower the heat and add the kale with about 2 tbsp of water so the kale steams and wilts down
5. Place it all in a serving bowl and add the pickled cabbage and the toppings you desire

Chapter 5: Kale Lunches

Kale is a fabulously versatile ingredient that not only provides you with many essential nutrients, but helps to fill you up without the bloated feeling you can get from too many carbohydrates. Eating kale at lunch time helps to provide stamina for the whole afternoon.

Kale, Potato and Chicken Soup

Makes enough for 4 servings

This hearty soup is perfect for those chilly days when you could do with something to warm you right through. For those who prefer a vegetarian diet, omit the chicken and use vegetable stock

Ingredients

- 6 cups of Baby Kale
- ½ a pound of diced Chicken Thigh
- 3 medium sized Potatoes
- 1 small onion
- 3 cloves of Garlic
- 1 quart of Chicken Stock or Broth
- 4 tbsp of Coconut Oil or Ghee
- 6 tbsp of Sour Cream
- Mint or Basil Leaves for a garnish
- Sea Salt and freshly cracked Black Pepper to taste

Directions

1. Wash the kale and remove any thick ribs or stems. Mince the garlic and dice the onion potatoes
2. Brown the diced chicken in a heavy bottomed saucepan with a little salt and pepper. Then remove and set aside
3. Sauté the garlic, onion and potatoes in the saucepan for about 5 minutes

4. Add the Chicken stock and return the chicken pieces to the saucepan and simmer for about 15 minutes or until the potato is tender

5. Add the baby kale and simmer until tender, about 2 to 3 minutes

6. Transfer the soup to your blender or food processor and pulverize it

7. Pour the soup back into your soup saucepan and taste it, adjust the seasoning if necessary, then serve it in soup plates, garnished sour cream and mint leaves

Kale Pesto Pizza

Makes two 9 inch pizzas or one, 12 inches

This pizza recipe uses the same pesto recipe described earlier and with additional kale and sun-dried tomatoes for the topping

Ingredients

- 1 pound of pizza dough, store bought or make your own by thoroughly mixing together a cup of flour, a tbsp. of yeast, a tsp. of sugar, a dash of salt and then add ½ a cup of lukewarm water and mix until smooth. Cover and set aside to rise for 30 minutes then roll out to the desired shape
- 2 cups of grated Mozzarella Cheese

- 2 tbsp of grated Parmesan (or any other tasty cheese)
- 1 cup of packed Kale with stem removed and torn into bite sized pieces
- 1 tsp of Olive Oil
- ¼ of a cup of thinly sliced Sun-dried Tomatoes
- ¼ of a tsp of fine Sea Salt
- Sea Salt and freshly Cracked Black Pepper to taste

Directions

1. Preheat your oven to 500F
2. Place the prepared kale in a small bowl and add the oil and salt. Then massage the oil evenly over all parts of the kale.
3. Roll out the pizza dough to your desired size and place in pizza pans or if you are using a pizza stone in oven, make the pizza on parchment paper to make lifting and transferring onto the hot stone in the oven easier
4. Top your pizza(s) with a nice even layer of pesto and sprinkle some Mozzarella on top, then add the kale and sun-dried tomatoes evenly over the pizza. Add a little more Mozzarella and Parmesan
5. Bake until the cheese on top is bubbling and the crust I golden brown
6. Slice and serve

Spicy Kale and Coconut Stir-fry

Makes enough for 2 servings

This flavorful, easy to prepare and cook stir-fry is reminiscent of dining in Thailand, it brings back fond memories of sunsets and clear water beaches.

Ingredients

- 1 large bunch of Kale with the thick ribs removed
- ¾ of a cup of diagonally sliced spring onions
- 1 small Carrot, sliced thinly
- 2 stalks of Celery
- 1 small Green pepper, sliced thinly
- 1 small Red or Yellow pepper, sliced thinly
- 4 Brussel Sprouts, sliced thinly
- 3 cloves of Garlic, minced
- 2 small fresh Limes
- A 1/4 inch piece of Ginger, finely sliced
- 2 Eggs, lightly beaten with a pinch of Sea Salt
- ¾ cup of large Coconut Flakes (do not use shredded)
- 2 cups of cooked Brown Rice
- 2 tsp of Chili Sauce
- 2 tsp of Tamari Sauce
- 1 tbsp of Oyster Sauce
- Coconut Oil or Ghee for cooking

- 1 handful of fresh herbs of your choice for a garnish

Directions

1. Heat your 12 inch wok or large fry pan to a medium heat and place in it 1 tsp. of oil. Cook the eggs until just set and then place them in a large bowl
2. Add about a tbsp. of oil in the wok and add the ginger first. Allow this to cook while stirring for about a minute, then add the garlic, carrots, celery, brussel sprouts and capsicum. Cook until just tender. Then place in the bowl on top of the eggs
3. Place 2 tsp. of oil in the wok and cook the coconut flakes until they are just golden brown, then add the rice stirring and cooking until heated through.
4. Once heated through, add the contents of the bowl back into the wok and add the chili, tamari and oyster sauces as well as the juice of 1 lime
5. Stir the mixture and serve in bowls with lime wedges and herbs as a garnish

Kale and Seafood Linguine

Makes enough for 3 to 4 large servings

The slightly bitter taste of the kale makes an enjoyable contrast to the sweetness of scallops and prawns and the spiciness of the Nduja (hot spicy salami). For those who are not partial to spicy foods, the nduja can be replaced with ham or cooked chicken.

Ingredients

- 3 oz. of Kale with the hard ribs removed
- ½ lb. of shelled Scallops with their roe
- ½ lb. of live Clams in the shell
- ½ lb. of live Mussels in the shell
- ½ lb. of shelled Tiger Prawns
- 8 oz. of Linguine or Fettucine
- 2 oz. of Nduja (soft hot spicy Salami)
- 2 cloves of Garlic, finely chopped
- 2 oz. of Dry White Wine (A nice drinking wine)
- 2 oz. of heavy Cream
- 2 tbsp of Olive Oil
- 1 small lemon, zested then cut into serving wedges
- Fresh Shaved Parmesan Cheese
- Freshly cracked Black Pepper

Directions

1. Cook the linguine until just under done in a large saucepan of salted water
2. Heat the olive oil in a large wok on a medium temperature and add the nduja. Break it up into the oil using a spoon, then add the garlic and cook until it becomes fragrant - about 1 minute
3. Turn up the heat and add all the seafood stirring to combine and after 2 minutes, add the kale, wine and cream
4. Place a lid on top and cook for about 3 minutes, then give a good stir. Remove any clams or mussels that did not open.
5. Drain the linguine and pour the sauce over it. Toss gently to combine. Stir in the lemon zest and garnish with the shaved parmesan, black pepper and lemon wedges

Chapter 6: Kale Dinners

Kale and Pork Casserole

Makes a serving for 4 people

Kale and pork casserole is a great comfort food, it satisfies our sweet, fatty and sour taste buds as well as making a filling meal.

Ingredients

- 4 cups of Kale with the stalks and ribs removed
- 1 pound of Pork Loin, trimmed and cubed
- 2 cups of Chicken or Vegetable Stock
- 3 cups of Potatoes, cubed
- 1 cup of Onion, Diced
- 1 cup of Carrots, julienned
- 3 cloves of Garlic, minced
- 1 tbsp of Paprika
- 2 tsp of Oregano
- 1 tsp of freshly made Mustard
- ½ a tsp of Chili Powder
- ¼ of a tsp of Black Pepper
- 1/8 of a tsp of Cayenne Pepper
- Coconut Oil or Ghee for cooking

Directions

1. Combine all the spices together and rub them into the pork so they completely cover the pieces
2. Place a heavy, bottomed skillet on a high heat and add the oil

3. When the oil is hot, add the pork a piece at a time and sear it on all sides (do not add too much or the juices will come out and the pork will boil becoming tough)

4. Cook the pork for about 5 minutes, then add the onions, carrot and Garlic and simmer for about 10 minutes

5. Add the potatoes and the broth

6. Simmer for about 25 to 30 minutes covered

7. Add the kale and simmer about another 10 minutes

8. Taste and adjust the seasoning if required and when the potatoes are tender serve

Cheesy Kale Casserole

Makes enough for 4 servings

This cheesy kale casserole is ideal for people who have not tried to eat kale before, it is a delicious and filling casserole that keeps well and can be frozen

Ingredients

- 10 ounces of fresh Kale with the stalks and ribs removed
- 1 pound of lean ground beef
- 2 cups of Marinara Sauce
- 4 ounces of Shredded Mozzarella Cheese
- 1 tsp of Garlic powder
- 1 tsp of Onion Powder
- 1 tsp of Oregano Leaves
- 1 tsp of Sea Salt
- ½ of a tsp of Ground Black Pepper
- 2 tbsp of Coconut or Olive Oil

Directions

1. Place the oil in a large, heavy bottomed pan on a medium to high heat
2. Add the beef when the oil is hot and break it up with a spoon so it does not clump together.
3. Continue cooking and stirring until all the beef is cooked, about 5 to 7 minutes

4. Then stir in the Garlic powder, onion powder, oregano, salt and pepper.

5. Stir the kale into the beef mixture and cook until it starts to wilt

6. Add the marinara sauce and continue cooking and stirring until it is all heated through

7. Add half of the mozzarella cheese and stir to combine

8. Sprinkle the rest of the cheese on top and place the casserole under an overhead grill (broiler) so the cheese melts

9. Allow the casserole to rest for 5 minutes, then serve

Marinated Beef and Kale Stew

Makes enough to serve 4 to 6 people

The stew has a deep, rich flavor from being marinated in red wine. The kale provides added vitamins as well as a nice contrasting texture. By stirring in some fresh squeezed lemon juice just before serving you will brighten all the flavors

Ingredients

- 2 large bunches of Kale, storks and ribs removed
- 2 pounds of Beef such as Chuck or Round Roast
- 2 Carrots, Large cubed
- 1 Large Onion, diced
- 2 cloves of minced Garlic
- 1 bottle of nice Dry Red Wine
- 10 whole Black Peppercorns
- 1 Bouquet garni made of 1 sprig of Parsley, 1 sprig of Rosemary and a Bay Leaf
- 2 cups of Stock of your choice
- Coconut Oil for cooking
- Sea Salt to taste

Direction

1. Place the beef, carrot, onion, garlic, wine, peppercorns and bouquet garni in a large food safe container and marinate

everything in the refrigerator for a minimum of 4 hours up to a maximum of 24 hours

2. Before you start cooking, first drain the stew by passing it through a colander into another container so you can set aside and retain the liquid to use later in the recipe

3. Place the beef cubes on paper towels and pat them dry, once dried season them with sea salt and pepper

4. Place a large, heavy bottomed stock pot on a medium heat and add 2 tablespoons of coconut oil. When the oil is hot, carefully place each piece of beef in the oil, leaving enough spaces between them so they will fry not boil in their own juices. This is an important step as if allowed to boil the meat will become tough and will not be as flavorful. You may need to do them in batches. Try to give each piece a nice deep brown crust all sides.

5. Place the meat once browned on a dish to rest while you cook the next batch. Once all the beef is browned and out of the stockpot, lower the heat and place all the vegetables in it

6. Cook the vegetables for about 5 minutes, stirring constantly to stop them burning and when they soften, add the browned beef, stock and marinade.

7. Simmer the stew stirring frequently and to deglaze the bottom of the pot

8. Simmer the stew for 60 to 90 minutes

9. About 15 minutes before the stew is finished cooking, prepare your kale, by tearing it into bite sized pieces, then add it to the stew.

10. Keep simmering the stew for about 10 minutes, the kale should be bright green and tender. Check the seasoning by tasting and adjust if necessary, then add a little lemon juice just before serving and enjoy

Kale, Chicken, Mushrooms and Noodles

Makes enough for 4 servings

This quick to make chicken noodle dish has crunchy beans, delicious mushrooms and tasty kale ideal for a quick weekend dinner. When cooking stir-fry, you need to work quickly so that nothing gets overcooked or cools down too much

Ingredients

- 3 oz. of Kale Leaves with the ribs removed
- 1 ½ lbs. of Chicken Breasts sliced into strips
- 1 cup of Green Beans, stringed and topped
- 1 ½ cups of Mushrooms, sliced
- 8 oz. of Udon Noodles
- 2 tsp of crushed Garlic
- 2 tsp of Chia seeds
- ½ a tsp of finely mince Ginger

Directions

1. Place a large wok over a high heat with a very small amount of oil and add your almonds tossing them rapidly or stirring constantly so they do not burn. They will become fragrant, very quickly about 30 seconds and then they should be removed from the heat and set to the side

2. In the same large wok, add a little more oil and cook your chicken strips so they are rare, not overdone. Once cooked, set them also to the side

3. Then once again in the same wok, cook your mushrooms, as soon as they start to soften, add the garlic and cook to al dente. Then remove from the heat and set it aside

4. Prepare your noodles in the manner suggested on the packet

5. While the noodles are being cooked or softening, Cook your beans in the wok. Use a little oil and toss them quickly, so they are bright colored and still crunchy

6. Add the chopped kale and chia seeds and stir them through.

7. Add back the chicken and mushrooms

8. Drain the noodles and carefully stir them through your chicken and vegetables

9. Serve the noodles on plates and sprinkle the almonds over the top or place in a serving bowl and add the almonds before serving

Kale Lasagna

Kale is terrific for adding substance and heartiness to this lasagna, giving it nutritional value and texture allowing for a new taste sensation.

Ingredients

- 1 large bunch of Kale, stalks and ribs removed, sliced in ribbons
- One 28 ounce can of whole Plum Tomatoes
- 1 cup of Roasted Red Peppers, diced
- 1 ½ cups of grated Mozzarella Cheese
- 15 ounces of Ricotta Cheese
- 2 large Egg Whites
- ¾ cup of sliced Mushrooms
- 2 cloves of Garlic, thinly sliced
- 9 sheets of no-boil lasagna noodles
- ½ a tsp of dried Oregano
- ¼ of a tsp of crushed Red Pepper Flakes
- ¼ of a tsp of Sugar
- 2 tbsp of coarsely chopped fresh Parsley
- 1 tbsp of Olive Oil
- Sea Salt and freshly cracked Black Pepper as needed

Directions

1. Place the tomatoes, peppers, oregano, ¼ of a tsp of salt, ¼ tsp of black pepper and the sugar into your blender or food processor and blender until the mixture is smooth, then set it aside
2. Mix together 1 cup of mozzarella cheese with the egg whites and the ricotta cheese and set these aside
3. Place the oil in a large pan or wok set on a medium to high heat.
4. Add the mushrooms and sauté until they release their juices and become tender
5. Stir in the sliced kale and as it wilts, add the garlic, pepper flakes and ¼ of a tsp of salt
6. Continue sautéing until the kale is totally wilted and bright green in color about 5 minutes
7. Preheat your oven to 375F

To assemble the lasagna

1. Lightly oil a 9 x 13 inch baking dish and spread ¾ of a cup of the tomato sauce, then place 3 of the lasagna sheets on top
2. Spread a layer of ½ of the ricotta and half the kale and mushroom mixture
3. Then another layer of lasagna sheet followed by another layer of tomato sauce, followed with lasagna and topped with the remaining ricotta and kale and mushrooms
4. Cover the lasagna with a lid or a sheet of foil and bake for about 45 minutes or until the sauce is bubbling around the sides and the noodles are tender

5. Remove the top or the foil and sprinkle with the remaining mozzarella cheese and bake under the grill to brown for about 5 minutes.
6. Allow it to stand for about 10 minutes, then garnish with the chopped parsley and serve

Kale and Portobello Mushrooms

Makes a vegetable serving for 4 people

Kale and Portobello Mushrooms make a great side dish to compliment any meal.

Ingredients

- 1 & ¼ pounds of Kale with the stems and ribs removed
- 4 Portobello Mushrooms, sliced
- ½ a cup of nice drinking, Dry Red Wine
- ¼ of a tsp of freshly grated Nutmeg
- 3 tbsp of Extra Virgin Olive Oil
- Sea Salt and freshly cracked Black Pepper as needed

Directions

1. Place a large, heavy bottomed frying pan or saucepan over a medium heat and add the olive oil
2. Add the mushrooms when the oil has become hot and sautee them until they are dark and tender
3. Add the kale and using tongs keep turning it until it wilts.
4. Season with salt and pepper
5. Add the red wine and use it to deglaze the bottom
6. Reduce the heat and simmer until the kale is tender and taste. Adjust the seasoning if necessary, then serve

Kale and Cannellini Bean Stew

Makes enough for 8 servings

Made using a Parmesan, garlic broth, this kale and Cannellini bean (or any other beans you like) is a medium to spicy vegetarian dish brings out the qualities of both **Ingredients**

For the Parmesan Garlic Broth

- 2 quarts of Vegetable Stock or Water
- 1 cup of Dry White Wine
- 1 pound of Parmesan Rinds
- 1 large Onion, finely diced
- 2 bulbs of Garlic with the cloves crushed
- A Bouquet garni made using 4 fresh Thyme sprigs, 4 fresh Sage Sprigs, 3 fresh or dried Bay Leaves and A dozen fresh Parsley sprigs
- 1 tsp of whole Black Peppercorns
- 1 tsp of allspice
- 6 whole Cloves
- ¼ of a tsp of Celery Seeds
- ¼ of a tsp of Coriander Seeds
- 1 tsp of Sea Salt
- 2 tbsp of Coconut Oil

For the Stew

- A large bunch of Kale with the hard stalks and ribs removed

- 1 cup of diced Carrots
- 1 cup of sliced Celery Stalks
- 2.5 cups of diced Onion
- 3 large cloves of Garlic, thinly sliced
- A 15 oz. can of diced Tomatoes
- 4 x 15 oz. cans of Cannellini Beans, drained
- ¼ of a cup of Red Wine Vinegar
- 8 thick slices of Bread
- Shaved Parmesan for the bread
- Red Pepper Flakes for a garnish

To make the broth

1. Place the oil in a large, heavy bottomed saucepan and sauté the onion, garlic and salt until tender and just golden brown.
2. Add the stock wine, Bouquet garni spices and Parmesan Rinds and bring to the boil. Then reduce the heat until you have a slow simmer. Simmer until the liquid is reduced by about half, approximately 2 hours
3. Strain the broth through a fine sieve and press to remove all the liquid. There should be about 4 cups and a little water if needed

To make the stew

1. Place the oil in a large, heavy bottomed saucepan and when hot, add the onions, carrots, celery, garlic as well as a large pinch each of salt and cracked black pepper. Sauté for about 10 minutes and then add the broth, tomatoes, beans and a little more salt.

2. Simmer the stew for about 15 minutes and taste it, then adjust the seasoning if necessary
3. Brush one side of the bread with oil and toast it, then brush the other side and put the shaved Parmesan on top before toasting.
4. Place the toasted Parmesan bread in each of your serving bowls and ladle the stew on top, garnish with the red pepper flakes and serve

Chapter 7: Dessert Ideas

Kale is not something you would usually think of to make desserts from, but this very versatile vegetable is extremely adaptable as the following dessert ideas will show.

Kale Ice Cream

Makes about 1 and a half Quarts

This very tasty vegetable ice cream is made using sweet potatoes, kale, cream cheese and spices.

Ingredients

- 5 cups of fresh Kale that has had the stalks and hard ribs removed, the is blanches in boiling water before being chilled
- 2 medium sized Sweet Potatoes, peeled and chopped in small cubes
- ¾ of a cup of Raw Sugar
- 2 cups of Half and Half or Cream
- 8 ounces of softened Cream Cheese
- 2 tbsp of Unsweetened Butter
- 2 tsp of Vanilla Essence
- ¼ of a tsp of Cinnamon
- ¼ of a tsp of Nutmeg
- 1/8 of a tsp of Sea Salt

Directions

1. Heat a large, heavy bottomed saucepan on a medium heat and melt the butter until it is totally melted
2. Add the sweet potatoes and ¼ of a tsp of salt and simmer them on a low heat covered for about 10 minutes stirring occasionally.

3. Then turn up the heat and cook them until they become very soft, they will need constant stirring to avoid burning. Continue cooking until they start to brown, then turn off the heat and allow them to cool slightly

4. Placed the cooled sweet potato in a food processor or blender and puree them with ¼ of a cup of half and half or cream. Then place them in a separate bowl

5. Place the blanched kale in your blender with the sugar, cream cheese and add the rest of the half and half as well as the spices. Blend this on high until well combined

6. Then blend the sweet potatoes, the kale and cream cheese mixture together

7. Season to taste with salt

8. Pass the mixture through a colander or fine sieve, then place in a food safe air tight container and place it in the freezer until it becomes very cold. Approximately 3 hours

9. If you have an ice cream maker, then churn it in that following the manufactures instructions

10. If you do not have an ice cream maker the alternative is to leave it in the freezer until it starts to freeze, then re-blend it to break up the ice crystals. It will have to be re-frozen and then blended several times.

11. Before serving, remove it from your freezer 15 minutes before serving and it will be easier use

Kale Cake with a Sweet Potato Filling

Makes 6 to 8 slices

This vegan recipe contains a small amount of sugar and is a great treat to end a meal or have as a healthy snack anytime.

Ingredients

Cake Ingredients

- 2 cups of Kale that has been blanched, cooled and finely chopped
- 1 cup of Walnuts, chopped up
- 2 1/3 cups of All-Purpose Flour
- 1 cup of Raw Sugar
- 1 cup of Coconut Oil
- ¾ of a cup of Water
- 6 tbsp of Flax Seed Meal
- 1 tbsp of Vanilla Essence
- 1 ½ tsp of Baking Soda
- 1 tsp of Baking Powder
- 1 tsp of Cinnamon
- ½ a tsp of Nutmeg
- ½ a tsp of fine Sea Salt

For the cake filling

- 2 Sweet Potatoes, peeled, diced and boiled, then blended until they are smooth

- 2 cups of Almond Milk
- 1/3 of a cup of Sugar
- 2 tbsp of Arrowroot
- 1 tbsp of Vegan Margarine
- 2 tsp of Vanilla Extract
- ¼ of a tsp of fine Sea Salt
- A pinch of Nutmeg

Icing Ingredients

- Two x 8 ounce containers of Cream Cheese
- ½ a cup of Vegan Margarine
- ¾ to 1 ½ cups of powdered Raw Sugar
- 1 tsp of Vanilla Essence

Filling Directions

1. Place the arrowroot and sugar in a heavy bottomed saucepan and whisk them together
2. Add the sweet potato and almond milk, then whisk this mixture until there are no lumps
3. Place the saucepan over a medium heat and continuously whisk it until the custard thickens to the point where, if you coat the back of a wooden spoon with the custard. Then run your finger through it the tail will not close up
4. When the custard is thick enough, remove it from the heat
5. Whisk in the vegan margarine, vanilla and the nutmeg
6. Place the custard in a new bowl with a plastic sheet placed right on the surface to prevent a skin forming there

Directions for the Cake

1. Preheat your oven to 350F
2. Line two 8 inch by 8 inch cake pans with parchment paper
3. Sift together the flour and salt to fully combine and aerate them
4. Whisk the flax seed meal and the water together in a large mixing bowl
5. Beat the sugar and oil into the flax seed mixture
6. Add the vanilla and blanched kale together and mix these until they are fully combined
7. Add the flour and salt mixture and stir this until it is completely moistened, then fold in the walnuts
8. Pour the batter equally into the two parchment paper lined cake pans
9. Bake them in the preheated oven for about 18 minutes or until, when you insert a toothpick into the center of the cake, it comes out clean

Icing Directions

1. Beat the cream cheese and vegan butter together
2. Add the powdered sugar and vanilla essence and whip this mixture just until it is smooth, but avoid over beating it
3. When the cakes have cooled, they will probably need to be loosened from the pans with a knife
4. Carefully lift the cakes from the pans using the parchment and then peel the parchment paper away from the cakes
5. Frost one of the cakes with the sweet potato filling mixture

6. Place the other cake on top of the frosted cake
7. Frost the top and sides of the layered cake with the icing mixture
8. The cake should be placed in the refrigerator to cool before serving chilled

Kale Ice Candy

Makes about a dozen, depending on the size of your molds

This ice candy treat tastes great and is also very good for you. Many people would be surprised that it contains lots of kale. The fruit can be pre frozen if preferred, we often freeze any surplus ripe bananas we have because they make great smoothies or can be used in these ice candies.

Ingredients

- 2 cups of Kale with the stalks and hard ribs removed
- 3 large ripe Bananas
- 16 whole Strawberries or any other sweetish Berry

Directions

1. Clean the strawberries by rinsing with a solution made of 2 tsp. of baking soda to a pint of water, this will remove any dirt or dust and also take away any wax or chemicals on the delicate fruit's surface
2. The kale should also be rinsed, you can use the same solution then fresh water
3. Peel the banana
4. Place all the ingredients in your food processor or blender and puree them until smooth. If you like a less smooth texture, just pulse them until you get the consistency and texture you desire

5. Once blended place or pour the mixture into freezer pop molds and freeze, then enjoy

Kale Chocolate Cake

Makes about 8 to 12 slices

This chocolate cake is very healthy so you can indulge without the need of feeling guilty or worry you are not being health conscious.

Ingredients for the Cake

- 3 cups of Kale with their stems and hard ribs removed, then finely chopped
- 2 cups of All-purpose Flour
- 4 ounces of Semi Sweet Chocolate
- ¼ of a cup of Cocoa Powder
- ¾ of a cup of Sour Cream
- 1 cup of Unsalted Butter at room temperature
- 1 ¾ cups of Raw Sugar
- 4 large Eggs
- 1 tsp of Vanilla Extract
- 1 ½ tsp of Baking Powder
- ¾ of a tsp of Baking Soda
- 1 tsp of fine Sea Salt

Ingredients for the Frosting

- 2 sticks of Unsalted Butter at room temperature
- 3 ½ cups of Sugar that has been sifted
- ½ a cup of Cocoa Powder that has been sifted
- ½ a tsp of fine Sea Salt

- 2 tsp of Vanilla Extract
- 4 tbsp of Full Cream

Directions

1. Lightly grease two 8 inch by 8 inch cake pans with butter, then dust them with cocoa powder
2. Place a saucepan with a little water on the heat to boil then place the chocolate in a bowl in the boiling water to melt. When the chocolate has melted, blanch the kale for 2 minutes
3. Then place the kale in your food processor or blender and puree until it's smooth (add a little water if needed). Then remove any fibers by straining the kale
4. Add ¾ of a cup of cooked kale to the chocolate and then add the cocoa powder
5. Add the sour cream and whisk it all together to combine
6. Beat together the sugar and butter until fluffy and light
7. Add in the eggs, one at a time, beating to combine before adding the next
8. In a separate medium bowl, whisk together the flour, salt, soda and baking powder
9. Mix together the cakes by adding the butter mixture and flour mixtures to the kale bowl to totally combine the batter
10. Preheat your oven to 350F
11. Pour the batter equally into the two parchment lined cake pans
12. Bake for 30 to 35 minutes, they are ready when you insert a toothpick into the center of the cake, it comes out clean

13. When cooked, take the cakes from the oven and allow them to sit for 10 minutes before removing and placing them on wire racks to cool

To make the Frosting

1. Sift the sugar and cocoa together
2. Cream the butter and add the sugar, cocoa, salt and vanilla extract together
3. The frosting will for after you beat this mixture for about 3 minutes
4. When the cake is completely cooled, frost the top of one cake, then place it on top of the other and frost the top and sides

Kale and Coconut Cream Pie

Makes enough for 4 to 6 servings

This rich and tasty kale and coconut cream pie will please even the most discerning or fussy eaters, it is simple yet complex flavor makes it suitable for any occasion.

Ingredients

For the Pastry

- 2 ½ cups of plain Flour
- 1/3 of a cup of cold Unsalted Butter, cut in small cubes and placed in iced water
- 2 large Egg Yolks
- 2 to 4 tbsp of iced water

For the filling

- 3 cups of Kale leaves with stalks and ribs removed
- 1 ½ cups of Whole Milk
- 1 cup of Coconut Milk
- ½ a cup of granulated Raw Sugar
- 2 large Eggs
- 4 tbsp of Cornflour
- 2 tsp. of Vanilla Extract
- 1/8 tsp. of fine Sea Salt

For the topping

- 1 cup of Whole Cream (whipping cream)
- 2 tbsp. of powdered Icing Sugar
- 2 tbsp. of Shredded Coconut

Directions

For the Pastry

1. Place the butter and flour in your food processor and pulse it until resembles breadcrumbs
2. Add the egg yolks, then pulse the mixture until it forms into a ball (add a very small amount of cold water if needed). Then place covered in the refrigerator for 30 minutes
3. Preheat your oven to 350F
4. Roll out the pastry to fit a 9 inch pie dish and place it inside
5. Place some parchment paper on the pastry and cover with cooking beans or raw rice and bake for 12 minutes to set the base
6. Remove the bean and paper and bake another 8 minutes, then cool

For the filling

1. Soak the dried coconut in 1/3 of a cup of the milk as leave to the side
2. Blanch the kale for 2 minutes, then cool in iced water
3. Then place the kale in your food processor or blender and puree until it's smooth (add a little water if needed). Then remove any fibers by straining the kale

4. In a small bowl, make a slurry using 4 tbsp of whole milk and the cornflour
5. Place the whole milk and coconut in a saucepan and bring to just under the boil
6. Whisk the sugar, eggs, vanilla and cornflour slurry together in a large bowl
7. Slowly add a small amount of the hot milk to the egg mixture while whisking to combine
8. Add the rest of the hot milk to the egg mixture slowly while whisking
9. Add the shredded coconut and milk as well as the pureed kale, then whisk to combine
10. Place the whole mixture back into the saucepan and cook on a low heat for about 6 minutes while continuously stirring until it thickens
11. Remove it from the heat and stir while it cools, then place it in a bowl and when cool, place it in the refrigerator to chill for 60 minutes
12. When cool, place the mixture into the pastry shell and refrigerate it again for several hours
13. Beat the Cream and icing sugar together until thick and then spread it on top and then sprinkle the shredded coconut and serve

Conclusion

With that, we have come to an end of this book. I hope you found the book informative and it has given you some inspiration and some good ideas.

You can use this book as a simple guide to understand the health benefits of kale and try to use them in your regular diet to ensure you stay healthy. Since kale is readily available in the local market as well as on online shopping sites, you can start adding them to your food recipes. The recipes in this book will ensure you consume ample quantities of this nutritious superfood. Don't restrict your creativity and get more innovative with your recipes.

Thank You!

Before you go, we'd like to say thank you for purchasing our book and congratulations for reading until the end.

If you found the book valuable, can you recommend it to others? One way to do that is to post a review on Amazon. Click Here to leave a review for this book on Amazon!

If you want to leave a private feedback, please email your feedback to: feedback@dingopublishing.com

Your feedback is important to us. We value and appreciate receiving your compliments or suggestions. Your feedback will help us continue to improve our books.

Free Gift

As a way of saying thanks for your purchase, we're offering a special gift that's exclusive to my readers.

Visit this link below to claim your bonus.

http://dingopublishing.com/heath-freebonus/

More books from us

Visit our bookstore at: http://www.dingopublishing.com

Below is some of our favorite books:

THE TOP 99 DELICIOUS RECIPES TO
FIGHT CANCER AND RESTORE YOUR HEALTH

ANTI-CANCER
Diet

Olivia Green

WHAT YOU NEED TO KNOW ABOUT FUCOIDAN & AHCC
UNDERSTAND THEIR BENEFITS AND SIDE EFFECTS FOR CANCER TREATMENT

ANTI-CANCER
Nutrients
FUCOIDAN & AHCC

Olivia Green

RAMEN
NOODLES COOKBOOK

The Top 50 Delicious
Ramen Recipes To Cook At Home

LINDA NGUYEN

THAI
Simple Cookbook

QUICK AND EASY AUTHENTIC THAI
RECIPES TO MAKE AT HOME

LINDA LY

BURN FAT AND BUILD LEAN BODY FASTER WITH
HIGH INTENSITY INTERVAL TRAINING

JOSHUA KING

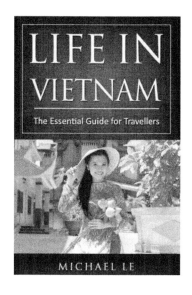

Sample chapters:

'Anti-Inflammatory Diet For Beginner'
by Jonathan Smith.

Introduction

These days, everywhere you go and every website you visit, you are going to find discussions or adverts about this or that diet program. Diets that can help you lose weight, diets that can cure cancer, and even diets that promise to increase your bank account. Some of these diets work; others are a waste of your time, energy, and financial resources. The anti-inflammatory diet is nothing like these fad diets. This revolutionary diet draws upon a simple scientific and biographical logic guaranteed to work for you regardless of your circumstances.

The anti-inflammatory diet has many innate benefits including lowering your risk of heart diseases, protecting the bones, helping you maintain a healthy weight, and increasing your body's ability to absorb nutrients from the foods you eat and the drugs you take.

This book is a comprehensive guide that shall impart upon you everything you need to know about the anti-inflammatory diet. Let's begin.

Chapter 1:
Introduction to the Anti-Inflammatory Diet

To make this book easy to read and follow, we will start by understanding inflammation and the anti-inflammatory diet.

In its simplest terms, an anti-inflammatory diet simply refers to a collection of foods that have the ability to fight off chronic inflammation in your body.

So what exactly is chronic inflammation?

Well, before we discuss that, let's start by understanding what inflammation is first.

So what is inflammation?

Inflammation is simply a term used to refer to your body's response to infection, injuries, imbalance, or irritation with the response being swelling, soreness, heat, or loss of body function. It is the body's first line of defence against bacteria, viruses and various other ailments. The goal is to 'quarantine' the area and bring about healing/relief. This is the good inflammation, as it is helpful to your body. It is often referred to as acute inflammation. However, there are times when the inflammatory process might not work as expected resulting to a cascade of activities that could ultimately result to cell and tissue damage especially if it takes place over a prolonged period. This is what's referred to as chronic inflammation. This type of inflammation has nothing to do with injuries; it is not as a result of an injury or anything related to bacteria, virus or any other microbe. And unlike acute inflammation that comes with soreness, pain, heat and swelling, chronic inflammation comes with another set of symptoms some of which include diarrhoea, skin outbreaks, congestion, dry eyes, headaches, loss of joint function and many others. This inflammation is what you need to fight using an anti-inflammatory diet because if it is not addressed early, it might result to a number of various chronic health complications that we will discuss in a while.

So how exactly does this chronic inflammation develop that would actually require a diet to undo? Here is how:

It all starts in the gut. The gut essentially has a large semi-porous lining, which tends to fluctuate depending on various chemicals that it comes into contact with. For instance, if exposed to cortisol, a hormone that is high when you are stressed, the lining becomes more permeable. The lining also becomes a lot more permeable depending on the changing levels of thyroid hormones. This increased permeability increases the likelihood of viruses, bacteria, yeast, toxins and various digested foods passing through the intestines to get into the bloodstream, a phenomenon referred to as leaky gut syndrome (LGS). The thing is, if this (the intestinal lining becomes damaged repetitively), the microvilli in the gut start getting crippled such that they cannot do their job well i.e. processing and using nutrients with some enzymes that are effective for proper digestion. This essentially makes your digestive system weaker a phenomenon that results to poor absorption of nutrients. If foreign substances find their way into the bloodstream through the wrong channels, this results to an immune response that could result to inflammation and allergic reactions. This form of inflammation can bring about different harmful complications. What's worse is that as inflammation increases, the body keeps on producing more white blood cells to fight off the foreign bodies that have found their way into the bloodstream. This can go on for a long time resulting to malfunctioning of different organs, nerves, joints, muscles, and connective tissues.

Chronic inflammation is harmful to your body and your brain. Let me explain more of this:

Your body is responsible for supplying glucose to your brain so that your brain can perform optimally. When you eat too much inflammation-causing foods, your body slows down its process of transporting glucose to the brain since it concentrates on fighting off the inflammation. Your brain then keeps asking the body for glucose since it is not getting its fill. This effect causes you to crave sugary and pro-inflammatory foods. Inflammation can also result to abnormal levels of water retention along with other problems that contribute to stubborn weight gain. This just worsens the condition and causes your inflammation to worsen. Unfortunately, majorities of dieters focused on weight loss only focus on reducing calories and fatty foods but pay very little attention to how eating pro-inflammatory foods may be contributing to an inability to lose weight quickly.

If inflammation persists, it can bring about a wide array of health complications some of which include:

- Obesity and chronic weight gain

- Lupus

- Arthritis

- Cancer

- Diabetes

- Celiac disease

- Crohn's disease

- Heart disease

So how exactly does inflammation lead to disease? That's what we will discuss next.

How Inflammation Could Lead to Diseases

It is possible to have a disease-free body, but only if you can manage to keep your body balanced. Diseases develop only when something upsets the equilibrium (balance) of the body. An abnormal composition of blood and nymph is a typical example of such imbalance. These two are responsible for supplying the tissues with nutrients and carrying away eliminated toxins, metabolic by-products and wastes from the liver and kidneys. When you consume unhealthy meals, it may affect the balance of blood and nymph in the body and lead to inadequate supply of nutrients and thus, the body would be unable to give adequate support to kidney and liver function. The consequence of this is that it exposes the body to the risks of several diseases and inflammatory conditions, which I mentioned earlier.

Food Allergies, Food Intolerance, and the Anti-Inflammatory Diet

Food allergies happen when your immune system reacts to the proteins in certain foods. Your immune system releases histamines that may cause production of throat mucous, runny nose, watery eyes, and in severe cases, diarrhea, hives, and anaphylaxis.

Your immune system's reaction to food allergies is to trigger inflammatory responses because when a food causes allergic reaction, it stimulates the production of antibodies that bind to the foods and may cross-react with the normal tissues in your body.

One of the highpoints of the anti-inflammatory diet is that it calls for the elimination of foods that promote allergies and intolerance.

How the Anti-Inflammatory Diet Works

To cure and stop incessant inflammation, you must eliminate the irritation and infection, and correct hormonal imbalance by eating specific foods while avoiding others. This would help stop the destruction of cells and hyperactive response of your immune system. When on an anti-inflammatory diet, most of the foods you shall be eating have powerful antioxidants that can help prevent and eliminate symptoms of inflammation.

For instance, anti-inflammatory foods such as avocados contain Glutathione, a powerful antioxidant. Radishes contain Indol-3-Carbinol (13C), which increases the flow of blood to injured areas. Pomegranates have polyphenols that stop the enzyme reactions the body uses to trigger inflammation. Shiitake Mushrooms are high in polyphenols that protect the liver cells from damage. Ginger has hormones that help ease inflammation pain.

We will discuss more on the foods you should eat and those you should avoid later.

In the next chapter, we shall look at the basic rules of the anti-inflammatory diet as well as how to get the best out of the diet program.

Chapter 2: Basic Rules of the Anti-Inflammatory Diet

As is the case with any diet, the anti-inflammatory diet has basic rules but as you are about to find out, these rules are very easy to follow and straightforward: no extreme rules that would leave you cravings-crazy and running back to a poor eating style after a few days.

When following this diet, there are about 11 rules you should follow:

1st: You Must Eat at Least 25 Grams of Fiber Daily

These should be whole grain fibrous foods such as oatmeal and barley, vegetables such as eggplant, onions, and okra, and fruits like blueberries and bananas. These fiber-rich foods have naturally occurring phytonutrients that help fight inflammation.

2nd: Eat at Least Nine Servings of Fruits and Vegetables Daily

A serving of fruit refers to half a cup of fruits while a serving of vegetable refers to a cup of leafy green vegetables. You could also add some herbs and spices such as ginger, cinnamon, and turmeric, foods that have strong anti-inflammatory and antioxidant properties.

3rd: Eat at Least Four Servings of Crucifers and Alliums Every Week

Crucifers refer to vegetables such as Brussels sprouts, Broccoli, mustard greens, Cabbage, and Cauliflower. Alliums refer to onions, garlic, scallions, and leek. These foods have strong anti-inflammatory properties and may even lower risks of cancer. You should eat at least four servings of these every day, and at least one clove of garlic daily.

4th: Consume Only 10% of Saturated Fat Daily

The average daily recommended calories for adults is about 2,000 calories every day. This means you have to limit your daily saturated fat caloric intake to no more than 200 calories. If you consume less than 2,000 calories daily, you have to reduce accordingly.

Saturated fats include foods like hydrogenated and partially hydrogenated oils, pork, desserts and baked goods, sausages, fried chicken and full fat diary. Saturated fats often contain toxic compounds that promote inflammation, which is why you need to eliminate these foods from your diet.

5th: Eat a Lot of Omega-3 Fatty Acid Rich Foods

Omega-3 fatty acids rich foods such as walnuts, kidney, navy and soybeans, flaxseed, sardines, salmon, herring, oysters, mackerel and anchovies are an essential part of this diet thanks to their strong anti-inflammatory properties.

6th: Eat Fish Thrice Weekly

It is important that you eat cold-water fish and low-fat fish at least three times a week because fishes are rich sources of healthy fats and can be great substitutes for saturated and unhealthy fats.

7th: Use Healthier Oils

The fact that you have to reduce your intake of some types of fat does not mean you should stop consuming all fats. You only need to reduce or even eliminate the consumption of unhealthy ones and limit your intake of healthy ones like expeller pressed canola, sunflower and safflower oil, and virgin olive oil. These oils have anti-oxidant properties that help detoxify the body.

8th: Eat Healthy Snacks at Least Twice Daily

Unlike in most diets, in this diet, you get to eat snacks as long as it is healthy. You can snack on healthy foods such Greek Yoghurt, almonds, celery sticks, pistachios, and carrots.

9th: Reduce Consumption of Processed Foods and Refined Sugars

Reducing your intake of artificial sweeteners and refined sugars can help alleviate insulin resistance and lower risks of blood pressure. It may also help reduce uric acid levels in your body. Having too much uric acid in your body may lead to gout, kidney stones, and even cancer. A high level of uric acid in the body is usually because of poor kidney function. Overloading your kidneys with pro-inflammatory foods may reduce kidney function and subsequently lead to excessive uric acid levels in the body.

Reducing your consumption of refined sugars and foods high in sodium can help reduce inflammation caused by excess uric acid within the body.

10th: Reduce Consumption of Trans Fat

Studies by the FDA reveal that foods high in trans-fat have higher levels of C-reactive protein, a biomarker for inflammation in the body. Foods like cookies and crackers, margarines, and any products with partially or fully hydrogenated oils are some of the foods with high trans-fat content.

11th: Use Fruits and Spices to Sweeten Your Meals

Instead of using sugar and harmful ingredients to sweeten your meals, use fruits that can act as natural sweeteners such as berries, apples, apricot, cinnamon, turmeric, ginger, sage, cloves, thyme, and rosemary.

Now that we have laid down the rules, the next thing we will do is to put what we've learnt into perspective i.e. what foods you should eat and what you should avoid. The next chapter has a comprehensive list of foods to consume and foods to avoid while on this diet. Consider printing out the chapter so you can use it as a reference each time you need to cook or make shopping decisions. If you do, it will not be long before you get used to the diet and can quickly decipher foods which foods you should and should not buy.

Anti-Inflammatory Diet for Beginner

By: Jonathan Smith

Find out more at:

http://dingopublishing.com/book/anti-inflammatory-diet-beginners/

Thanks again for purchasing this book.

We hope you enjoy it

Don't forget to claim your free bonus:

Visit this link below to claim your bonus now:

http://dingopublishing.com/heath-freebonus/

Printed in Great Britain
by Amazon

31141598R00056